The Aroma of Vanuatu
Four years of adventures in the South Pacific

Author: Mercedes López –Tomlinson

Foreword by Ana Briongos

The Aroma of Vanuatu
Four years of Adventure in the South Pacific
by Mercedes Lopez-Tomlinson
©of this edition 2019 Trotamundas Press Ltd.
book and cover design by Sonia Griñó
soniaibiza@gmail.com

Published by Trotamundas Press Ltd.
www.trotamundaspress.com
trotamundassite.wordpress.com
info@trotamundaspress.com
Trotamundas Press is an international publisher specializing in travel literature written by women travellers and adventurers and those who have experienced and written about other cultures apart from their own.
The aim of Trotamundas Press is to make available the culture and traditions of the different countries in the world to enable a greater understanding of our diversity and also of our similarities.

The Aroma of Vanuatu
To Peter, my companion for life
and adventures.
To Sonia, Rosa, Laura and Indira whom I
hope will be able to share adventures with
their aunt in the future.
To María, my grandmother, who left her
home in search of a better world.

FOREWORD

From ancient times, human beings have felt the need to visit lands far away from their homes.
Travellers across history have left a record of what they saw, and especially of those things that surprised them. Traders, soldiers, priests, and adventurers were nearly always men; although there have also been women, usually in the shadow of the former, in smaller numbers, and always reduced to a lower status: wives of conquerors and government officials, with the occasional intrepid nun and audacious lady explorer.
Travel writers have come from different countries situated in very different locations across the planet. Chinese Buddhist monks, who travelled westwards, and arrived at the Buddhist monastery of Bamiyan in Afghanistan, where they were surprised by some giant gleaming Buddhas that welcomed the passing caravans of travellers from their urn-like pedestals in the mountains. Greeks and Romans, like the famous Herodotus, followed their conquering armies, and described

their exploits, and the places through which they travelled. Arabs, like Ibn Batutta, who headed towards the Orient, and arrived at the court of the Mughal Emperor, Akbar the Great, in India, where he was received by the Emperor in person, and at whose side he remained and worked as a jurist for many years. The Spaniard, Ruy de Clavijo, who reached the court of the Great Khan in Samarkand, and left us his writings about all he saw there, along with Genovese and Venetian merchants, like Marco Polo. The British, with their colonial vision of the World, arrived in India, initially alone, but were later accompanied by their wives, some of who also became writers, though with their Victorian morality. Spanish conquistadores, who sailed across the Atlantic, left us their chronicles about the New World. European travellers with perceptions based on oriental studies, and Americans with a more modern outlook, only seemed to appreciate the exotic aspects of the countries they visited. Travellers of today from wealthy countries, who being burdened by a troubled conscience, only see poverty and filth when they move far away from the surroundings more familiar to them. Tourists, who travel as consumers of pre-fabricated, dense itineraries, make lightening visits during which they see and photograph, but do not observe, so that they can add to their list of destinations visited.

There are writers who have recounted the anxiety that certain curious people experience and that leads them to abandon the comfort and security of home and family, in spite of the difficulties and dangers, in order to throw themselves into an unknown world to see what it has to offer them. I think of the beautiful children's story by the Persian writer, Samad Behrangui, "Mahi e siá e kuchulú" (The Little Black Fish) that in the form of a modern parable, tells of how a small black fish, that lives quietly with his mother at the bend of a river, decides to venture down river in order to know other waters and their inhabitants. His adventure is like that of so many restless young people with a desire to get to know the world, as the personalities that he gets to know form a "bouquet" of human archetypes in the guise of inhabitants of the river and marine world, covering all the possible characteristics: generous, wise, intelligent, evil, greedy, etc.

In general, travellers have been well received wherever they have arrived because they came with news, innovation, foreign objects, new methodologies, and knowledge about remote places. In countries where women are segregated, women travellers have been the only ones to have the opportunity to enter and stay present in their private spaces, and to exchange information, ideas, hopes and feelings with them. I still remember, with emotion, my visits to the kitchen of the house of a judge in Kandahar in Southern Afghanistan, where his mother and wife told me happily that the gentleman of the house had chosen a new wife, and that soon there would be an extra woman to help with the housework, tell stories, give birth to more children, and participate in their education. He had had to give a fortune to the father of the girl in order that he would let go of her, and give her away in marriage. By contrast, when with great interest they had asked me, I had to confess that men were not going to pay anything for me in Spain, which for these women meant that I must have some hidden defect so as to have no value. This was their conclusion and my surprise.

These days, when torrents of information reach us from powerful communication media, accustomed to being biased, and at the service of obscure interests, the traveller, man or woman, provides, through his or her commentaries, the vision of the ordinary citizen. This vision of the things that the traveller sees, and the things that happen, can definitely go unnoticed by professional reporters in search of a story. This book by Mercedes López-Tomlinson is the result of several years of her life in an island in the Pacific, Vanuatu. Before her, another Catalan, Aurora Bertrana (1892-1972), daughter of the well-known author, Prudenci Bertrana, wrote a book Ocean Paradises (1930) about her stays in the exotic places of the South Pacific.

Her spontaneity and freshness, plus the exotic nature of the topic, earned her considerable success. Domènec Guansé considered that "the innocent sensuality running through the book was the feminine equivalent of the intended pantheism of Prudenci Bertrana." Three-quarters of a century later, Mercedes López-Tomlinson returns to the topic with a modern focus, as times have changed. The exotic no longer engulfs her, and neither do our eyes see those places labelled "exotic" in the same way as they were seen years ago. The realistic vision of Mercedes introduces us to a society where indigenous people and foreigners live side by side through their adventures and misadventures, and brings us a delicious read.

Ana Briongos

INTRODUCTION

From 1989 to 1993, I lived in Vanuatu in the South Pacific. It became an independent country in 1980. Before then, it was a colony governed by England and France, and used to be called the New Hebrides.

For those that do not know where it is, Vanuatu is a group of 83 islands set in a Y-shaped that are to be found between Australia and the Fiji islands. Vanuatu is surrounded by coral, and has one of the few active volcanoes in the world on the island of Tanna. Even so, the only things that the ni-Vanuatu (the indigenous inhabitants) fear are the cyclones and earthquakes that lash the islands every so often.

My four years of residence in this country were full of unusual anecdotes, special friendships, and unforgettable experiences in a part of the world that I consider myself privileged to have been able to get to know.

Recently, an English friend sent me a copy of an article published by The Guardian newspaper in

July 2006 about Vanuatu being considered the happiest country on Earth according to a drastic new index elaborated by the New Economics Foundation (NEF) and the Friends of the Earth. Soon after, a friend from Barcelona sent me another article about the same subject. I am convinced that heaven on earth does not exist, but for me, Vanuatu comes closest.

Although my dream as a child and as an adolescent was to travel to foreign lands, the more exotic the better, I never thought I would go so far. I always wanted to travel, but to live in the Antipodes exceeded my expectations. It is only now, as I put things into perspective that I realise what a great gift life has offered me. And like the best gifts, I have learned to appreciate its real value with the passing of the years.

I wish to remember these years that were full of light and new experiences, and bring back those marvellous scenes that had been stored away in a dusty drawer of my memory. I would like to think that in writing this book, I may be able to challenge the imagination of the reader, and transport them to a unique and special place that really exists.

Some of the people that I knew back then are no longer with us, but their journey through this world has not been in vain, as their memory is alive within me today as much as it was then. The trail that they left behind has contributed to make this world a better place than it would have been if they had not existed.

I have changed a few names for reasons of privacy, but all the stories that are included in this book are real life experiences, even if some cases they appear to be the fruits of a vivid imagination. I can testify that, in many cases, reality surpasses fiction, and this is one of those.

Mercedes López Tomlinson

ACKNOWLEDGEMENTS

My thanks are many, but I wish to expressly mention the people without whom this book would never have existed. The order in which mentioned is only of relative importance.

Special thanks to Peter Tomlinson, my partner in adventures and misadventures, because partly thanks to him, I went to live in the South Pacific. To my friend, Jo Hatcher, for being a friend from the distance during all these years since we met in Vanuatu. To Maritza Hawkins, for her loyal friendship during all these years. To Marta Riudeubás, my childhood friend, who came from Barcelona to Vanuatu in a crucial moment in her life, and with whom I could share unforgettable experiences in that marvellous place. To Mary Ann Crompton and Steve Myhre for their friendship and those marvellous Christmas parties at their incomparable house with views of a tropical lagoon in the South Pacific. To Caroline Forsyth. To Nikenike Vurobaravu, and his sons, Sale and Garae. To Lizzy, To Nerry Taurakoto. To

Colleen Wallis. To all those other people I knew in Vanuatu, and to whom I owe a debt of eternal gratitude for the lessons I learned from them.

Thanks to Myriam Dornoy-Vurobaravu, sorely missed as an inimitable and unforgettable human being. To departed friends, Ricard Iserte and Roger Taylor. To my father, José López Neira, who died a few hours after having telephoned me from Barcelona to wish me a Happy New Year. To my late uncle, Antonio Parés Neira, who died a few months before my return to Barcelona, and who, I'm sure would have found Vanuatu a fascinating place.

A special thanks to Ana Briongos, a great traveller and a charming friend, for encouraging me to put on paper my experiences in those marvellous islands. I wish you hours full of adventure and emotion is those marvellous far distant lands. Don't stop dreaming! Sometimes dreams become reality!

Mercedes López Tomlinson

Welcome to Paradise

We arrived in Vanuatu in November 1989. There had been various months preparing for the journey from London where I had been living since 1978. I went there from my native Barcelona to escape the constraints of Franco's dictatorship and Spanish society of that epoch.

In 1989 it was five years since I had married Peter, and one of the things that I liked about him from first meeting him, was that he spoke Spanish, which meant that both he and I knew the language and culture of the other, and I would not have to make efforts to teach him my mother tongue, or other things about my culture, so different from his.

I already knew London and the English culture very well. I studied English since I was ten years old, and before meeting Peter I lived there for three years working with English people, and handling things in that environment.

Peter, for his part, had just returned from Panama where he had worked for two years as a volunteer with a development organization in Santiago de Veraguas, the birthplace of Omar Torrijos (the Panamanian dictator).

I liked the fact that he had spent two years of his life helping the development of people in another country. Besides, in his profession of Chartered Accountant, it was a rare case amongst his contemporaries, because, in general, they are more interested in careers involving high finance than helping their fellow man.

My adventurous spirit had found her twin soul, although both of us took some months to realise this.

After several years in London, we felt ready to take a leap towards other parts of the world. One day, Peter mentioned to me that he had seen an advertisement asking for experts in his field to train local public servants in a country called Vanuatu. The name was so exotic, and neither he nor I had the faintest idea where it was!

We started to look at maps and could not find it. Finally, we discovered that it was a country in the South Pacific that used to be called the New

Hebrides before its independence in 1980, and the maps had not yet updated its name!

They received his curriculum vitae, and after several interviews, Peter got the job, which consisted of working for the Overseas Development Administration of the British Government to provide expertise and training for the officials of Vanuatu's Cooperative Department with the aim of building the capacity of ni-Vanuatu (native people of Vanuatu) so that they would be able to take charge of their country without the need for foreign experts. That was the idea.

We spent several months organizing our departure and deciding what we were not going to take with us for the two years that we were going to be living in Vanuatu. Then, we spent a week learning about the culture of Melanesia and the South Pacific. In those days I felt reluctant to go to a castle in the English countryside to get to know the ins and outs of Melanesian culture, but it turned out to be one of the best things I did in order to know better, and consequently adapt myself more easily to my new life.

I remember an anthropologist, who knew the South Pacific profoundly and with affection, and who explained to us that for the Melanesians, it is important not to offend people. For example, if a flight is cancelled and this would be upsetting for us, it is better that they don't tell us, which may leave us waiting for hours in a small airport in the jungle without anyone so kind as to inform us that the aeroplane is not going to arrive that particular day!

On the other hand, in Melanesian culture, lying is practically unknown, or at least, it was so in the period when we were living there. So for example, the police have an easy time to catch the suspect of a crime, because they only have to ask the person if he or she is guilty and the reply is an honest one. There is another particularity of Melanesian culture. Each time that you meet your brother-in-law you should tell a joke, the same joke, and he must always laugh. These small details are important to know in order not to become too confused in what, at the beginning, is totally different and unknown.

During the week at the castle, I also met a Catalan, who had been a correspondent and head of the Spanish language service of the BBC. Since retiring, he dedicated himself to preparing courses, like ours, to help British officials understand the situation and culture of the country where they would be living for several years. He told me that after the Spanish Civil War. he took his chance to escape and ended up in England. There he practiced his profession and established his life, but never forgot his mother tongue, and still spoke perfect Catalan.

In a different period, I had also escaped Barcelona and a hostile atmosphere in search of new horizons. I had grown up in the shadows of Franquismo that acted as a poisonous presence in my life. I needed fresh air with more freedom and greater openness, and I needed a place where I could be happy without having to explain myself to anybody.

At last, the emotional moment arrived for us to travel towards a world, unknown and exotic, and we felt ourselves on cloud nine, and impatient to arrive there.

We travelled to Los Angeles where we stayed one night in an enormous four star hotel near the airport, and after a bad experience with a mad taxi driver, we longed for the time when we could escape from that place.

Later, when we asked at the hotel reception where we could go for a stroll and become familiar with the area, the receptionist looked at us with horror, and said that she would not dare take a step outside the entrance to the hotel, except to go to her car!

In truth, we realized what the receptionist meant when we dared to try and cross the road to go to the bank, and we needed to run without waiting for the traffic lights to change, because there was a guy who was threatening us with what appeared to be a plastic gun.

From Los Angeles we departed for New Zealand. We arrived in Auckland, a city full of boats and yachts and wide avenues with wooden houses that could be transported to another location together with their inhabitants.

In Auckland, we stayed with a former colleague of Peter's time in Panama, and his Panamanian wife, with whom we visited the lovely region with thermals springs. They received us with great hospitality and these few days were a very pleasant introduction to this new part of the world. From Auckland, we left for our final destination, Port Vila, the capital of Vanuatu.

Several years have passed, but for me, the moment I left the plane to walk down the steps is something I will never forget. The mouthful of air, hot but not suffocating, and the view of the palm trees swaying in the smooth tropic breeze under a sky of bright red mixed with dark blue, was for me love at first sight for the place that would be my home for the next four years.

I believe that we arrived on one of the most beautiful nights that I had seen in my entire life, even though I was born and grew up in the Mediterranean. We were received at the airport by a gentleman, a native of Vanuatu, who spoke perfect English and was the director of the department where Peter was going to work. He was very charming and offered us a warm welcoming smile that made us feel that our arrival was really welcome. He accompanied us to the hotel, where he bid goodbye, and left us to rest, ready for the next day, which was to be full of new experiences for us.

Peter and I stayed alone together in the hotel room. We looked at each other and started to laugh for joy and happiness. We had arrived as close to paradise as we knew. It was only the beginning of an unforgettable adventure.

The French, the English and the Natives – Together but not mixed

The first few days in Vanuatu were a constant discovery. I could not stop being surprised how in a small city of 15,000 inhabitants, as was Port Vila in 1989, there could be such a variety of languages and races, although Melanesian was the predominant one. In the street, one could see Polynesian, Chinese, Vietnamese, Caucasian and Melanesian people, plus others with a mixture of these races. In Vanuatu, there existed 130 languages for a population of only 180,000 distributed across 83 islands.

As a result of past English and French colonialism, every ni-Vanuatu spoke at least three languages, one was the mother tongue, or the language of their island, another was bislama, a creole language that was created with a mixture of influences including English, French and even some Spanish words, and the other was English or French depending on which school they had studied at. The ni-Vanuatu, who speak fluently English or French, or both, plus their mother tongue and bislama, have an ability to learn languages and normally speak several languages.

On a normal day, I found myself speaking French in the French supermarket, English in the post office and Bislama in the market, as well as Spanish with people from the small Latin American community that lived in Port Vila. Languages have always been my great passion and I am very lucky to have an aptitude for them.

I gave Spanish classes at the University of the South Pacific as part of the Faculty of Foreign Languages, and at the French Lycee, plus the French School of Vanuatu. Amongst all the students that I taught, the most outstanding were the Vietnamese and the ni-Vanuatu, much more than the children of the English and French colonisers. Little by little, I was discovering the mysteries of a fascinating culture that opened up slowly like a book whose subject fascinates and, at the same time, challenges one to value new ways of understanding life.

The colonial past of Vanuatu is one of the keys to understanding the reticence that the ni-Vanuatu have about fully trusting people of other races, especially white people.

The name of Vanuatu is a recent creation. It is the name the country was given for its independence on 30 July 1980 and means "Our eternal land". Before then, Vanuatu was known as the New Hebrides, the name that Capitan James Cook gave it when he reached the islands in 1774, maybe in memory of the Scottish Hebrides Islands.

Prior to James Cook, Pedro Fernández de Quirós, who although Portuguese, was a Captain working for the Spanish crown, reached these islands in May 1606. However, constant skirmishes with the natives forced Quirós and his sailors to flee the islands after only 55 days. We must not forget that apart from the diseases and the hostility of the natives, cannibalism was widely practiced on the islands. Nevertheless, Quirós left a legacy with the name of the first island he discovered, Tierra Australia del Espíritu Santo (Southern Land of the Holy Spirit). Today, the island continues to be known as Espiritu Santo, familiarly known by all as 'Santo'.

French explorers also reached Vanuatu. The legendary Bouganville arrived in 1768 and Laperouse, another famous explorer, came in 1778. However, both ships sank in the coral reefs during violent storms, and there were no survivors to tell their tales, and the islands remained uncharted on the maps for another century.

The islands were rich in sandalwood, a very valuable timber in the Eighteenth Century. There was also copra. Copra is the pulp from coconuts and is used to make coconut oil. Whalers arrived on the islands, followed by traders, who extracted all the sandalwood trees from the forests. At the same time, the missionaries arrived, determined to covert the Melanesians, who lived on the islands, to Christianity. In reality, it was a mixture of traders and missionaries that were the Europeans who first arrived, eager to exploit their riches, and full of adventurous zeal in the face of the unknown.

In 1906, the archipelago of 83 islands that formed the New Hebrides was declared The Condominium of the New Hebrides. The French wanted to take the country from their base in New

Caledonia, meanwhile the British wanted to do the same from their bases in Fiji and Australia. This conflict of interests led to the creation of a joint system of dual government: French – British. This meant that there were two types of systems for all things. To loop the loop, the judge at the court was a Spaniard, appointed for his neutrality by the French and the British. The Count of Good Hope (El Conde de Buena Esperanza - in Spanish) happened to be deaf and his knowledge of English and French was sparse!

When I arrived in Vanuatu in 1989, one could still see the inheritance of a dual colonial past: the French restaurants with the best wines imported from France, the banks from New Zealand and Australia, the Burns Philp supermarkets that had been founded by a Scot one hundred years ago, and Hebrida, the French supermarket in which one could find tins of escargots on the shelves and butter imported from France in the delicatessen.

I also remember a shop called 'La cave du vin' with a selection of French wines worthy of envy by any self-respecting wine cellar in France. In this context, the wines of Australia and New Zealand were considered second class. French snobbism knows no frontiers. I was told a curious anecdote: when a criminal was sentenced to jail, he was allowed to choose between the English or the French prison. Nearly every one of them chose the French prison because the food was better.

Continuing with the subject of colonialism, Vanuatu is a country with ancient traditions that go back as much as three thousand years, and they still persist. On some islands, even today, the presence of a Caucasian man or woman can stir up mass flight and even fear amongst the natives.

During the Nineteenth Century, thousands of islanders were forcibly taken from their islands, and obliged to work on sugar plantations in Australia or Fiji. Sometimes, they were convinced through trickery, promising them rewards that later were not provided, and they ended up working in similar conditions to those of slavery. In cases where the deception did not produce the desired effect, they were kidnapped and held in chains on the boats until the destination country,

as if they might have been slaves, even though slavery was abolished in 1867. Very few of them survived in order to return to their islands and recount their experiences, but those that did left a legacy of terror about the boats of white people.
I have already commented earlier that these islands have traditionally practiced cannibalism. Sound proof of this comes from the American explorers, Osa and Martin Johnson, on a visit to the islands in 1917 when they had to flee Malekula because the chief of the 'Big Nambas' tried to capture them in order to eat them. In the Port Vila museum there is a photo of the Johnson couple with the well know cannibal chief of the most feared tribe.
Cannibalism disappeared officially in the 1960s, and it is difficult to believe that in such recent times such an ancient tradition may have been eradicated. It is doubtful that it no longer exists. The large iron pot situated at the entrance to the Port Vila Cultural Centre is a record of this recent past of cannibalism.
At that time, television did not exist in Vanuatu, and on the only radio station, which did not take

advertisements, tamtams (traditional drums) were sounded to indicate a change of programme. I remember that once the sound of the tamtams continued for nearly an hour, and I asked Lizzy, my assistant, why it was that they sounded for such a long time. She replied that they were passing messages between islands that only the islanders could decipher, so that the white people would not understand the content of the message!
It is a country full of colour and contrast. The population is principally of Melanesian race, the same race that inhabits other countries of the region like Papua New Guinea, the Solomon Islands and New Caledonia. Although nowadays in the capital, Port Vila, one can see different races that arrived on the islands in different eras.
There are white settlers, descendants of the French and English, who colonized the islands in the Nineteenth century, and one can also see Chinese and Vietnamese, who arrived as workers on the copra plantations, plus Polynesians emigrating from other South Pacific islands. , In more recent times, people from Australia and New Zealand

have settled.

But the Vanuatu of thousands of years continues to have its roots in the other islands of the archipelago. It is there where life continues largely unaltered for thousands of years. It is difficult to understand that there are civilizations that still exist and have not changed their ancient rhythm, but Vanuatu is the exception that proves the rule.

The British Ambassador

In January 2006, I received a call from a friend that I had met in Vanuatu and about whom for several years I had not known anything. We spent a weekend together remembering old times in my house in Italy, where I now live.
Mary Ann told me that she had been appointed Consul General for the New Zealand Embassy for the United Nations in Geneva, and she called me to tell me that we were going to be living at a short distance. Everything is relative, because from Turin to Geneva is a three and half hours drive, but we promised to see each other as often as our lives allowed. Her visit brought me many memories. We met in a curious situation in Port Vila, and even today, I laugh when I remember the circumstances.

In 1989, Vanuatu, with only nine years of independence after the end of the Franco-British Condominium of the New Hebrides, swarmed with foreign diplomats and technocrats that were living in the country with contracts of two years, renewable for up to six years.

As Peter was working as a technocrat under a contract with the British government, we were invited to a dinner at the residence of the British High Commissioner a few days after our arrival in the country. We were received by the High Commissioner, Kevin Johnson, who as soon as I introduced myself, and knowing that I was Spanish, made the following comment: "So you are from Spain. You have very cheap wines there!" to which I not being submissive responded: "I think you must have been mixing with the wrong crowd there." With this beginning, it promised to be an exciting dinner.

Kevin Johnson, I thought, matched the image of an ambassador like an elephant to an ant. During the welcome cocktail, I was briefly introduced to other diplomats and technocrats, like us, and then the moment came to move to the terrace of the mansion for dinner. I checked and found that I was seated at the table of the High Commissioner, and, to top it all, right next to him.

As is customary in diplomatic circles, recent

arrivals are allocated to the tables of the head of mission and of his (or her) spouse, who sit on separate tables. This serves to get to know more about the recent arrivals and to find out their opinions on life in general. As I later found out, there was a rumour among some expatriates that Kevin Johnson was a spy working for MI6, the same service for which the famous fictional character, James Bond, is employed, although they could not be more different. At least James Bond was handsome and had good manners.

Mary Ann and Steve were seated at the same table. At that time, Mary Ann was the First Secretary of the New Zealand Embassy, and Steve, a sculptor in the Maori tradition, was her husband and official companion at these dinners. During the course of the dinner, Kevin Johnson addressed Mary Ann commenting that it was a great piece of luck for New Zealand to have been colonized by the British, who, according to him, had brought civilization to a previously uncivilized land. Then he left his mark by saying: "And look at you, Mary Ann, you are a good example of what I mean."

My friendship with Mary-Ann started when I heard her reply: "Perhaps you should know, Kevin, that I have Maori ancestors, of whom I am extremely proud." At that moment, Kevin Johnson behaved like a true ambassador and changed the subject, but uncomfortably as if his body suffered from St Vitus dance, though, at the same time ,resigned to not having the final word on this occasion.

During the dinner, I had the opportunity to converse with Mary Ann and Steve and this was the start of our great friendship. We began to organise picnics on deserted beaches where we used to go with a group of 6 to 12 people, and enjoy the incomparable beauty of unspoilt beaches and coconut palms without company, except our own. However, one needed to be careful, because if at the entrance to the beach there were strewn branches from a sacred tree, then is was totally forbidden to pass with having the authorization of the local chief, who would normally give the necessary permission in return for a small gift or payment. Otherwise, one risked the fury of the local population, who could slash the tyres of the cars without being observed by anybody. In the end, they were right. It was their beach and we were the visitors.

We always used to bring snorkelling masks as the waters were full of colourful fish and coral. It was essential to wear rubber shoes to avoid the risk of getting cuts from the coral that are impossible to cure except if you immediately apply lemon or lime juice to disinfect them. How many weekends full of lasting memories with unforgettable friends under the tropical sun in the South Pacific! It seemed to us that the problems of the world did not exist in those moments and the beauty that we enjoyed filled us with positive energy that recharged our batteries. I can truly say that during the four years I spent in that part of the world, I managed to forget what it feels like to be depressed. I also never encountered anyone who showed symptoms of depression.

We celebrated two Christmases with Mary Ann and Steve at their marvellous house from which you could view one of the two tropical lagoons of Port Vila, and the island of Erakor. These were the Christmases that I remember with the greatest fondness because of the excellent company, and the unequalled panoramas.

The sunsets visible from our house remain some of the most spectacular that I have seen. We watched them closely from our lovely house in Malapoa situated on the high part of a hill leading out of Port Vila from where we could see the island of Iririki in the distance, and the boats that arrived at the port. I feel a little nostalgia when Christmas comes around, and I remember those that we spent with unforgettable friends in the tropics of the South Pacific.

A toast with kava and other Melanesian customs

There are no street children, nor orphans, nor abandoned children in Vanuatu. This is not because the children do not suffer abuse, or because parents do not die, rather it is because, in Vanuatu, children do not only belong exclusively to their mother and father, but are members of the family group that includes uncles, aunts, grandparents and cousins.

If the family group considers that it is not in the interests of a boy or girl to remain with their parents for whatever reason, another member of the family will take care of him or her. If the behaviour that caused this decision changes, then the children can return to their parents, but, if not, there will always be another member of the family to take care of them. The children call various members of their family, mummy and daddy, even if they do not live in the same house.

If a couple cannot have children, the family clan will give them a child because this child will always remain within the family group. All this implies a different set of sociological beliefs to those of our Western society where the child is considered the exclusive property of the biological parents, and it is difficult for the authorities to allow another member of the family to take care of them, even in cases of continuous demonstrated abuse. For example, I cannot go to the house of my brother and take his children from him, so to speak, even if I know that they are not well look after. By contrast, in Vanuatu, the family members have the right, and the duty, to do so for the welfare of the child.

As a consequence of all this, delinquent children, abandoned children, and abused children do not exist, or at least, there are very few cases. This is one of the things that we should respect about, and learn from, Melanesian society. Sometimes, we are not aware that there are things that do not function well in our society, but in another function better. Melanesian tradition also has a flip side of the coin. For example, if a Melanesian man or woman tells you that he or she very much likes the watch you are wearing, it is considered bad manners not to give it to him or her. This applies to all objects, and therefore one needs to take great care when saying that you like something that belongs to another person, because they may feel obliged to give it to you. Later, they will take their revenge and ask you for something of yours in return.

I remember once that a Melanesian friend commented to Peter that he very much liked his shirt. As Peter also liked the shirt, he had to search everywhere in order to find an identical one, and finally he found one that was similar, but he had to give away his original one to his Melanesian friend. Fortunately, it was only a shirt!

Another feature of Melanesian culture is that the more you have, the more you must distribute between the members of your family. The concept of "this is mine and that is yours" does not exist within family groups. So if you have been saving up to buy a car, and your cousin comes along and asks you for a loan (without specifying what for), you have to give him your money, that is if your cousin knows that you have some. The promise to repay will always be given, but is rarely fulfilled.

In the case that you do not follow the rules, you risk being rejected by your family group, an immeasurable disgrace in Melanesian terms.

My friend, Lucia, wife of an anthropologist and expert in Melanesian customs, commented to me that the most miserable shack in a village sometimes houses someone secretly rich. That person pretends to be poor in order to prevent his relatives from taking everything. This made me think of Mr Chiang Shen, who had a home appliances and general store in Port Vila. He had arrived from China at the age of 14 in order to work in the shop of a relative, and over the years had opened his own store that overshadowed the one of his uncle. Mr Chiang always dressed in short trousers full of holes and a torn t-shirt, but it appears he had invested in several houses in the centre of Sydney, that had appreciated in value to be worth millions of dollars. This is a case of how appearances can be deceiving. In this way, he also protected himself from any kind of request for credit. Although this person was born in China, he had adapted perfectly to the Melanesian culture,

following many years of residence in the country.
As a Melanesian, you have to take these things seriously because, if not, they can change your life. The shopkeepers of Vanuatu know very well that when relatives arrive from far away asking for loans, they will never see the money again. They have to make sure the cash till is empty in case the relatives wish to check if it is true that nothing was sold that day.
On the other hand, if you fall on hard times, your Melanesian family will make sure that you do not die of hunger, and you will always be welcomed in the houses of relatives that you call upon, asking for something to eat, or somewhere to sleep. It is a society of solidarity that respects blood ties and abides by the motto "today for you and tomorrow for me".
The land is also an ancestral right. Everybody possesses a more-or-less large piece of land to cultivate, and consequently hunger does not exist in such a fertile land. Land cannot be sold as private property, but passes from generation to generation in the same family, which considers

itself a guardian of its allocated land to conserve it unspoilt to pass the land on to future generations. Only in special cases will a small piece of land be allocated to a member of another clan or tribe.

In this respect, the white colonisers caused big problems because they sought to become property owners of lands about which the Melanesians considered themselves to be mere custodians for future generations. For the Melanesians, land is not a commodity that can be bought and sold. Land has been given to a family to use and cultivate, and maybe construct a house, but later it must pass to a future generation.

Since independence in 1980, plots of land can be leased for long periods at reasonable prices, and therefore an expatriate may build a house, but he or she will never become the owner of the land upon which it is built.

One has to understand the rules of the game, and not break them, because, if not, one risks suffering the consequences. All this applies to Melanesian society, and to the Westerners who marry into it. My French friend, Myriam, who was married to a ni-Vanuatu, and therefore part of the family group, told me that some nephews of her husband, that lived with them, would take her jewellery and give pieces to their girlfriends, or wear them themselves. She was not able to do anything about it because personal property within the family clan does not exist. Myriam always wore a bracelet that had belonged to her grandmother, and other objects that she did not want to disappear. For the rest, she gave up.

For Myriam, who never had a good relationship with her own mother, her mother-in-law had become the mother she never had had, so to say. She had been totally accepted in the family group based on the fact that her husband had married her, and this was reason enough to benefit from all the love and solidarity that exists in the majority of Melanesian families. At the same time, her children had various members of the family that they addressed as mummy and daddy, and Myriam knew that if anything were to happen to her and her husband, her children would always be protected and looked after within the core of the family. That's not bad for a society considered unsophisticated according to Western thinking.

Another curious Melanesian tradition is that the groom must pay a price for the bride. This can be paid with pigs, which are very important in Melanesian culture, or with kava, a traditional narcotic drink, or with jute mats, or, in the case of a non-Melanesian, in cash. In the event of not paying the bride price asked for by the bride's family, the groom risks terrible consequences that range from being poisoned with a potion prepared by a sorcerer, through to being rejected by the family group and expelled from it, and losing all rights over the wife.

Pigs are a very important part of Melanesian culture. The wealth of a Melanesian is measured by how many pigs he possesses. They are used in traditional ceremonies, and are eaten only after having been slaughtered during graduation ceremonies to move to a higher status in the community. To reach the different grades and to become a "chief", one has to kill many pigs, and each ceremony to reach a higher status involves the slaughtering of pigs, and a banquet to eat them. Pigs are considered to be a source of wealth for their owners, and have more value than women for the majority of men in Vanuatu. The pigs of Vanuatu have tusks that coil around their cheeks and that, later on, will be converted into precious bracelets that denote a certain status. However, currently it is possible to purchase them in certain artefact stores in Port Vila so that tourists can take one home as a souvenir. The most valuable ones are those that have several coils, and are only worn by chiefs of the highest status.

Kava is a drink traditionally used in ceremonies and rituals. It is a narcotic with a taste that is frankly disagreeable. In the past, women were not allowed to drink kava, nor stay near to the nakamals, (traditional bars for kava) where the Melanesians meet to drink it and communicate with their ancestors.

Kava has some interesting effects. It paralyzes the body but not the brain, which continues to remain lucid. People who drink kava regularly do so to relax the body, although the mind stays awake as normal. Something like a drunk, who moves with difficulty, although in reality he is mentally sober, but is incapable of demonstrating this.

Kava continues to be used in rituals, and it is considered rude for a westerner not to drink a shell of kava (you drink it in coconut shells cut in half) during formal events such as inaugurations, weddings, etc.

I was told a story that describes very well the westerner's mind's perception of kava. There was a ceremony of inauguration for a very important building, like a new ministry or something similar, and the dignitaries present included the members of the diplomatic corps, who were resident in the country. A welcome cocktail was served and then the speeches commenced. The ni-Vanuatu master of ceremonies started to fill the coconut shells with kava from a bucket that had been placed at his side.

The moment for toasts arrived, and it was the turn of the Australian ambassador to make a toast, and then the British ambassador, the French one and on and on until eventually the turn of the ni-

Vanuatu minister came. This latter had to make a great effort to hide his disgust with the drink. In all cases, the ni-Vanuatu do not wish to be embarrassed, or to make others feel embarrassed, and therefore he drank the liquid in the shell.

At the end of the ceremony, the minister spoke to the organizer of the banquet and told him of his disgust with the drink served that was certainly not kava. It was then discovered that someone had mixed up the washing up bucket with the bucket that contained the kava. The ambassadors had drunk the watery detergent without saying anything!

Several of our friends were kava drinkers. The ritual of kava starts at sunset, which in the tropics is around 6pm. When it gets dark, one goes to the nakamal where the kava drinkers meet in silence to imbibe the drink. It is like a bar but with silence. They also invite each other to shells of kava, but after three or four, the body will no longer move and absolute silence reigns amongst the drinkers, even though their minds are wide awake.

The majority of kava drinkers organize a family

member or friend to come and pick them up and take them back home, a difficult task in the case of someone with a few kilos extra who needs support in order to walk. Sometimes, one sees cars travelling at 10 kilometres per hour, and it was evident that the driver had recently been to a nakamal.

They say that kava is not addictive, and does not have side effects, but I am not convinced of this, because kava drinkers are very punctual in keeping their appointment at the nakamal as soon as the sun dips below the horizon and the moon rises. That moment is sacred and if you wish to find someone, you know where to go, the nakamal that is open that evening

The history of kava is as old as the culture of these islands, meaning thousands of years. The drink is obtained by fermenting the root of the plant, and in the case of very sacred rituals, it is chewed by young virgins and spat into a bucket. Kava roots are an important part of the bride price, along with pigs, and the jute mats that cover the floors of the traditional huts. It is always part of any ceremony or ritual.

The nakamal is the definitive meeting place and gossip hub on the islands. Today, women are accepted, but are not any better regarded than women who drink alcohol in our society.

For a few years, I understand, kava has been produced commercially and kava pills can be found in pharmacies in the United States. I have heard that famous Hollywood actresses are fans of kava, saying that it is healthier than valium. Moreover, it is a laxative, which helps to lose weight moderately.

Southern Land of the Holy Spirit (Espiritu Santo)

Santo is one of the most beautiful places on earth to practice scuba diving, and this is one of the most popular activities for the expatriate community in Vanuatu.

The island of "Santo", as it is popularly known, was the first island to be discovered by Pedro Fernández de Quirós in 1606 in the name of the Spanish crown, and he named it Espiritu Santo (Southern Land of the Holy Spirit). It is the largest island in Vanuatu. Its land area is around 4,000 square kilometres, with Mount Tabwemasana lying on the western side of the island. The eastern and southern parts are flat, and full of copra plantations and cattle ranches.

Santo is full of surprises that one discovers little by little, and these contribute to the numerous legends featured in books like 'South Pacific', which made way for the famous musical of the same name. It was written by James Michener after he was stationed in Santo as a soldier during the Second World War.

The famous island of Bali-Hai that features in the book by James Michener, was inspired by the real island of Ambae, from which, it is said, come the most beautiful women in Vanuatu. I can imagine James Michener contemplating the island of Ambae in the distance during the fantastic sunsets, and dreaming of the story that would later take shape in his book.

Santo was famous during the Second World War as the military base for 100,000 American troops. In a country, which had only 120,000 inhabitants spread over 83 islands, this represented a very important occurrence. The Americans left many buildings that still exist today, plus various landing strips, and three dive sites that are unequalled anywhere else in the world.

One of the most wildly desired dive sites for divers across the world is the ship 'President Coolidge' that sank after hitting a naval mine and lies practically intact starting at 20 metres depth. It is the largest sunken shipwreck accessible to scuba divers in the world. Another important place for diving is the shipwreck of USS Tucker, which is situated in a maritime channel.

Million Dollar Points is the place where the Americans jettisoned their war supplies, vehicles, and telecommunications equipment, which they had wanted to sell to the Condominium of the New Hebrides. The government of the New Hebrides had refused to purchase this equipment, perhaps believing that the Americans would abandon it, rather than transport it back to their country, but the Americans decided to throw it into the sea. At the time, this was one of the most significant ecological disasters that anyone could remember, but today it is a protected ocean park and a paradise for divers.

In amongst the dense vegetation of the jungle, one can find the remains of aeroplanes that disappeared during the war. When I lived in Vanuatu, aircraft also disappeared and it proved difficult to locate them in the jungle vegetation, if they were ever found at all.

I remember a plane crash, in which various people that I knew in Vanuatu, perished. One of them came from a famous British family, and the tragic incident was reported in the most important English newspapers.

I remember once having dinner with Cassie Clunies- Ross at the residence of the British High Commissioner soon after she arrived in Vanuatu to work as a development volunteer, and as luck would have it, we were seated at the same table. In spite of belonging to a famous family, I found her to be natural and friendly, as the British say. I liked her simplicity, and the fact that she wore a skirt and blouse, apologising for not having brought anything more elegant. After all, she was a young woman in her twenties, who had come to work as a volunteer.

Later on, I learned that she had been going out with a French photographer, who was very well known for his shots of the ni-Vanuatu people, their dress and make-up during Vanuatu rituals. I have one of his photos, taken during the famous Toka dance from the island of Tanna.

Another person, who died in this accident, was Andrew, a young Australian diplomat, whom I had met at various parties, and who had got married just one month before. He had boarded the plane at the last moment, almost forced to do so by the others "because it was going to be a grand adventure that he should not miss". This is what he had told his wife during their last telephone conversation. They were going to take photos of remote places. In fact, he only had one more day on Santo, and was due to return to Port Vila the next day.

The news of the accident had a strong impact on the expatriate community. It could have been anyone of us to be a passenger on that plane. The rescue teams took more than a week to find the plane wreckage lost in the dense jungle. It was a funeral with tears, rain and much emotion. All of us were affected one way or another. Life is very fragile, and I realised the truth of this in Vanuatu.

In Luganville, the capital of Santo, one can still see some buildings that were built by the Americans during the Second World War, and still in use today without significant changes to their structures.

The beach called Champagne Beach is where the Americans celebrated the end of the war, and, as the name implies, rivers of champagne flowed that day. It is also one of the most spectacular and beautiful beaches in the South Pacific. I was swimming in its crystal clear waters and trying to imagine how this nearly deserted beach was once full of American soldiers celebrating the end of the war in one of the most enchanting places on earth.

Santo was also the scene of famous incidents during the war for independence in the late 1970s. The most famous is the one with the secessionist leader, Jimmy Stevens, as the main protagonist. He was a ni-Vanuatu of mixed Melanesian-Scottish blood (his father was a Scottish colonial settler and his mother was Melanesian), that attempted to declare independence for the Independent State of Vemerana, with the support of the Nagriamal conservative movement that was promoting a return to a traditional lifestyle, which included the right for men to have several wives at the same time (polygamy).

Jimmy Stevens was a charismatic hero, who had pushed for the independence of the country at the United Nations in 1971, which had led to the creation of the Anglophone Vanua'aku party led by Father Walter Lini. By contrast, the majority of Francophone ni-Vanuatu were against the idea of independence.

England and France administered the so-called Condominium of the New Hebrides. Both competed for power and influence. As I have mentioned, many Francophones, and, particularly those of mixed French-Melanesian race, were against independence. Some wanted the continuation of the condominium, whereas others sought an annexation by France as an overseas territory.

In this confused scenario, the first general elections debates took place, and the secessionist leader, Jimmy Stevens, also participated by seeking the independence of Santo.

In November of 1979, the Anglophone Vanua'aku Party of Father Walter Lini won the majority of the votes, which did not mean that everyone was in agreement. One has to remember that Vanuatu has 83 islands and more than 113 different languages. It is one of the countries with the most diverse cultures in the world.

When Jimmy Stevens raised the flag of the Independent State of Venerama in Santo, and he declared himself prime minister, there was no support for his government from either the French or the English, who were abandoning the country. Walter Lini could not do anything, because officially he had not yet taken power. He had to resort to asking aid from the army of independent Papua New Guinea in order to control the situation.

It was known as the Coconut War by the news media of the epoch. It ended when the son of Jimmy Stevens died as a result of bullet wound incurred when he jumped a roadblock. Jimmy Stevens issued a statement in which he asserted that he had not wished things to go this far, nor hurt anyone, and he surrendered unconditionally. Later on, some documents came to light in which it was indicated that the French administration, although officially supporting Walter Lini as the elected representative of the people, secretly preferred the secessionist supporters of Jimmy

Stevens.

Jimmy Stevens spent the last years of his life as a patient in Port Vila hospital where he was the most charismatic patient and known to everyone. He could be seen there in lively conversation with other people. It was not that he was permanently sick, but the hospital was better than his designated cell in the prison.

One evening in the month of June 1980, the flags of Britain and France were lowered and, in the midst of emotion and tears, the flag of the new nation of Vanuatu was hoisted aloft. At last, Vanuatu was free of its colonial past. Vanuatu commenced a new beginning to retake the reins of its own destiny, although it would not be easy.

The Island of Pentecost and Bungee Jumping

Every island in Vanuatu has its traditions and celebrations. Some of these are unique and unknown to the rest of the planet, while others have been converted into spectacles that are far removed from the original tradition.

For certain, few people know that the origin of Bungee Jumping (jumping into the air from a high structure whist attached to a long elastic cord) comes from the island of Pentecost in Vanuatu. Pentecost was discovered in 1768 by the French explorer, Louis de Bouganville, who named it as such for having been sighted on that day.

For more than 2,000 years, the men of Pentecost carry out each year one of the most spectacular rituals ever known. As soon as the first yam (a root vegetable that forms part of the traditional diet) harvest commences, the men build wooden towers that can reach up to 27 metres in height.

During two consecutive days of celebrations, accompanied by ritual songs and dances, various men, chosen by each village on the island, climb the tower and jump into the air with their ankles attached to vines that prevent them from crashing into the ground below. The vines have to be 10 centimetres shorter than the height of the jump so that it will not be mortal

A jumping ritual, which is undertaken without problems, assures a good yam harvest for the following year. The dates of the ritual have to be endorsed by the tribal chiefs, and it is considered to be bad luck not to follow this practice. One of the very rare occasions when a man died from jumping occurred during a visit to Vanuatu by Queen Elizabeth II of England during the 1970s.

Going against local custom that holds it to be inauspicious to organise the jumps on dates that have not been endorsed by the tribal chiefs, the advisers to the Queen of England wished to include in her visit the opportunity to see such as unusual ceremony as the Pentecost land diving. The man who undertook the jump crashed into the ground because the vine around his ankle broke. This took place in the presence of Her Majesty the Queen of England.

According to popular legend, the jump takes place in memory of Tamalie, who was the victim of his wife's cunning. It is said that men fertilize the soil when they touch it with their shoulders during the land dive. The first jump was initiated by Tamalie's wife, who refused to consummate the marriage and ran away from her husband, who anxiously chased after her. In trying to escape from him, the woman climbed high up a tree, and when her husband tried to reach her, she leaped into the air. At the same time, Tamalie leaped after her, but he was killed as he crashed into the ground below, whereas his wife survived unhurt because she had tied the vines from the tree around her ankles. Ever since then, tradition requires that only men are to be the ones to jump into the void with vines attached to their ankles.

These traditional customs and values have been maintained for centuries, and the ni-Vanuatu are proud of this. It is not only a series of rituals, ceremonies, and traditions, but also a way of life. The ni-Vanuatu culture, or kastom (in Bislama), sets out how to behave and, together with the traditional customs, is a source of unity between the people in order to live in peace and harmony. There are traditions that, as the society changes, have evolved or disappeared, but, in general, the majority of the customs are maintained in order to protect and guide the ni-Vanuatu across their earthly passage.

There was a time when white colonialism threatened to destroy "kastom" and it was feared that this would happen. Currently however, the government, as well as the church leaders, and the tribal (clan) chiefs recognise the need to maintain ancestral traditions. One has to bear in mind that Vanuatu is a country where the Prime Minister includes a magician amongst his bodyguards to protect him from his enemies.

The National Council of Chiefs, called Malvatumauri, was established to protect the ni-Vanuatu customs, culture and traditions. Malvatumauri was founded on 27 April 1977 and all the tribal chiefs from all the islands are represented. One of its main functions is to advise the government on all questions related to kastom, culture and tradition.

A president, elected unanimously by all the chiefs, with an office in the capital Port Vila, represents the National Council of Chiefs. Every year, there is a public holiday on 5th April to celebrate the day of tribal chiefs. The chiefs help to maintain peace and harmony between the different communities (clans) on the 83 islands that form the archipelago, through respect for the ancestral traditions and customs, including Christianity.

The Bungee jump of Pentecost Island is an expression of the thousand years old culture of these islands, whose name means "Our Eternal Land."

The island of Tanna and its volcano

There are places that we keep in a box of unforgettable memories. I visited Tanna several times, and clearly recall each one of my trips. It is, for me, one of the islands that reminds me most vividly of the spirit of the Melanesian soul of Vanuatu.

The island of Tanna is one of Vanuatu's most populated. At the same time, it is one of the most fascinating. On Tanna, traditional culture and kastom, or traditional rules for coexistence, prevail, and, sometimes, it is hard to believe that we were there at the end of the Twentieth Century. Captain James Cook was the first European to discover Tanna in August 1774, after having seen a reflection of the volcano Yasur in the sky. His ship, HMS Resolution, arrived at a bay that he named Port Resolution that it still retains today.

The Nineteenth Century was characterised by many battles against foreigners. Missionaries, in particular, encountered many difficulties, and in many cases, were killed and then eaten in the

cannibal feasts that predominated in that epoch.
My friend, Marta, came to stay with me for a month in 1991. Her husband, Andrew, had died in strange and painful circumstances and this journey was to a place unknown to her, far away from the painful memories of Barcelona. I believe that in those moments of Marta's life, Vanuatu represented a pain relief balm for a wound accumulated over the previous months. She was very brave to accept my invitation to pass some weeks on the other side of the globe from Barcelona. I hope that she still remembers those days as healing for her emotional wounds that helped her to keep going.
One of the most impressive trips to the island of Tanna was to the Yasur volcano. In those days, it was still possible to climb up to the crater of the active volcano. It is an unforgettable experience to behold a crater full of lava. We climbed the sheer slope up to the rim of the crater without anyone else around, except our ni-Vanuatu guide.
Arriving at the top of the crater, we look down to behold fireworks and a mass of smoke, continuously changing colour. It felt so very near, but the flames

did not reach us. This was something both unique and impressive.

Many villages on Tanna retain their traditional lifestyle since thousands of years, and one can still see houses built in trees, men wearing the traditional namba, a loincloth made with leaves from the Pandanus tree, and the women, bear-breasted with traditional grass skirts. The latter is very different to the traditional "Mother Hubbard" dress that the missionaries introduced in the name of modesty, which, in terms of attire was an essential part of their teachings.

In Port Vila, the capital, the majority of ni-Vanuatu women use the modest "Mother Hubbard" dress, and one has to travel to the islands to see the more traditional type of clothing. The dress covers the woman's body from the neck down to the calves, and is made of cotton with floral motifs that I have only seen in the South Pacific.

On Tanna, there are many traditional dances and ceremonies throughout the year, but one of the most spectacular is the Toka ceremony. The festival lasts three days, and the village in charge of organizing it tries to surpass the efforts of the previous village in terms of food and gifts. Traditional gifts are pigs, the principal source of wealth, kava, the traditional drink, and straw or jute mats, which are used to cover the floors of the huts. There is a kind of beauty contest during the festival that motivates the men, as well as the women and children, to paint their faces in the most picturesque ways.

In my house, I have a photo by the famous French photographer resident in Vanuatu, Philip Metois, of a woman dressed and painted for the Toka ceremony that reminds me vividly of those days. I am sure that these ceremonies continue to be celebrated in the same ancestral fashion year after year.

One time on a visit to Tanna, I stayed in the house of an Australian colleague of my husband, who was married to a woman from Papua New Guinea. Her pet was a crazy goat called Tommy. That goat cornered me in the kitchen without letting me move an inch, and in a very threatening manner. I remained like that for what seemed like an eternity, but was probably ten minutes, until Dora, the owner of the animal, rescued me. From that moment onwards, I don't remember a second when I was not looking around on all sides before moving about in the house or the village.

I found out some months later that Tommy, the goat, had died, poisoned by a neighbour. His owners were in deep mourning. I felt a little ashamed to feel some level of relief in thinking that the goat would no longer be waiting for me on my next visit to Tanna.

I have always found the people of Tanna to be welcoming and friendly. I remember a little girl called Serendipity, who immediately made friends with me, and, who, within a few minutes of knowing me, brought me a beautiful shell of a sea snail that she had found on one of the beaches. I still have it, and it is one of the most precious items in my small collection.

On Tanna, I knew that I could move around the island without danger. Maybe, this was because I was the invited guest of Yarkin and his family. Through my husband, Peter, who worked as an adviser to the local cooperatives, I had access to the local people and, as a guest, I received all the respect and hospitality that they were able to offer. One of the aspects that I consider most picturesque about the mentality of the people of Tanna is their adherence to the so-called Cargo Cults. These cults have their genesis in the strange mentality of the Melanesians, so different form our own. One of these cults that exists on Tanna, is called 'John Frum'. This cult's origin traces back to the Second World War, when the Americans had a huge base with 100,000 soldiers in the New Hebrides.

Maybe, the fact of seeing black soldiers with the same power as the whites, and the fact that in reality there did exist a soldier called John, played their part. Ever since then, there has existed a cult on Tanna that has the symbol of the Red Cross, and holds a big parade annually, awaiting the return of 'John Frum' with many gifts for everyone.

For the members of this curious cult, there will be riches for all his followers the day that 'John Frum' returns, and they will be forever young and rich. It is no surprise that with such promises, the cult has followers. The Melanesian mentality is very literal, and so, for example, when, during the Second World War, they saw soldiers of the same colour as themselves driving all-terrain vehicles, drinking all the Coca Cola that they liked, and using all types of equipment, the Melanesians concluded that they too could have access to all that. This explains the birth of the cult.

Another very peculiar cult existing on Tanna is the Prince Philip (of England) Cult referring to the Duke of Edinburgh. It so happened that on Tanna, it was discovered that there was a European man (Prince Philip) married to a very powerful woman (the Queen of England), and being something very unusual, since women in Vanuatu are considered less valuable than pigs, they concluded that he was a supernatural spirit with magic powers.

When the British District Agent of the era (we are talking about the 1960s), Mr Wilkins, was due to visit London, the village men presented him with a gift for Prince Philip consisting of a ceremonial mallet for killing pigs designed for a chief of superior status. When Prince Philip received the gift, he asked Mr Wilkens to convey his gratitude to the people for the present, and sent them a signed photograph of himself.

Upon his return and owing to the imprecise nature of the message passed on by Mr Wilkens, in addition to the photograph, the men of Tanna concluded that Prince Philip was expressing support for their beliefs. From then on, they took this as confirmation that the Prince was the personification (re-birth) of an ancestral spirit as is part of Melanesian culture.

A curious situation arose when Prince Philip visited the islands with the Queen of England in the 1970s. His advisers asked him not to visit Tanna because, if he did so, the followers of his cult would put into action the cult's beliefs, which would cause a collective chaos since all marriages would be null and void, and the women would become fair game for all the men according to their desires.

Followers of the cult can still be found today moving around the island dressed in loincloths, and exhibiting the signed photograph of Prince

Philip of England. In Vanuatu, reality is stranger than fiction.

Another memory that I conserve from Tanna is that of swimming with a dugong, or sea cow. It appears that the dugong had decided to stay in one of the bays on Tanna, the place where he had arrived with his mate, who had died shortly after their arrival at Port Resolution. Sometimes, and only when it appealed to him, he used to accompany the people, who went to swim in those parts. This was our case, and almost without us noticing, we felt the dugong swimming at our side. This was a unique and unforgettable experience, and it is very unlikely to happen twice.

Every stay on Tanna took me through to a different era compared with the relatively western influenced civilization that one found in Port Vila. It was like being in a time machine and going back several hundreds of years.

Contrasts from Vanuatu

This chapter reproduces an article that I wrote, and which was published unchanged in El País Internacional (the international edition of the leading Spanish newspaper) on 21 December 1992 as a celebration of its 500th edition. The editors of El País had written to me asking for my opinions about such a remote culture. They dedicated a half page to my article without altering the text I had written. It was titled 'Contrastes desde Vanuatu' ('Contrasts from Vanuatu') and expressed in a few words the experience of living in these islands. A few months later, I returned to Barcelona.

Each time that I read it, I reflect on the relevance of certain events in the panorama of the current world situation, with only the names changing. Unfortunately, we continue not to learn the lessons of history.

Here is the article.

It was quite a surprise to receive your recent letter asking for my impressions about EL PAIS, Edición Internacional from such a remote place.

I will try to describe, to the best of my ability, my experiences and impressions when I receive your newspaper, which I hold in high esteem.

I believe that when one has not had the opportunity to live, like me, on some very remote islands, that preserve a many thousand years old culture, it is difficult to imagine that something so accessible in other countries as international news, is, for me when I receive El PAIS, one of the few points of contact with what is happening in the rest of the world. However, sometimes, after reading the news, I feel very privileged to be able to stay so distant from a so-called civilization that seems to do no more than pass from one war to another.

My ni-Vanuatu (indigenous people of Vanuatu) friends have trouble believing that the images of children starving to death are real. Here, food is considered to be a fundamental right for all human-beings and is never denied to anyone, either in the form of a plate of food, or a piece of land where a person can grow vegetables. They treat children with a lot of care. "Why do they permit this to happen in their countries?" the people here ask me. Unfortunately, I do not have any valid answers for this question.

However, I continue to miss all the news about my country and the world, and, thanks to EL PAIS, the newspaper helps me to keep my heart nearer to Spain and Europe through their adventures and misadventures.

It would be difficult to find another newspaper so ecologically well used as my copies of EL PAIS. Though I am the only Spaniard in this place, I am not the only Spanish speaker. Here there is a spectrum of people of all colours who speak Spanish. In the first place, after my husband, who although British also speaks Spanish, and I read the newspaper, I pass it on to other interested people, who in turn give it to the library of the University of the South Pacific, where I give Spanish classes.

In my classes, I use articles taken from EL PAIS for reading exercises and to initiate a discussion. The most recent article that I used was about the Seville Expo, with the anecdote that when I asked my students if they would like to have visited the Expo, one Ni-Vanuatu lady replied yes, but she was afraid of "being trampled underfoot by so many people". One has to take into account that this is a country with 130,000 inhabitants distributed over 80 islands surrounded by coconut palms and coral reefs. The capital has 15,000 inhabitants and for some people, who have never left their own island, this is considered to be a huge agglomeration of people.

I do not know if it would be of interest to know that the first discoverer of these islands in 1606 was a Spaniard, Pedro Fernández de Quirós, (in reality he was Portuguese, but he worked for the Spanish crown) who, for certain, did not last long in this place, as after various skirmishes with the natives and the disappearance of the majority of his crew, owing in part to malaria and in part to cannibalism, he had to rapidly raise anchor. In any case, the names in Spanish of some island remained from his short visit, such as Espíritu Santo, familiarly known as Santo.

Yet I find it difficult to believe that during the three and a half years that I have been living here so many unexpected things have happened in the world. I missed the dismantling of the Iron Curtain in the countries of Eastern Europe, the ugly increase of a mean and obtuse nationalism, and a tepid resurgence of fascism that makes me think that history has not taught us enough to avoid committing again the errors of the past. Added to all this is the civil war in Yugoslavia in that same European continent.

Next year, I will return to Barcelona, my city of birth, and I only hope that my transition from this society, so pure and tranquil, to the asphalted urban jungle will not be too hard.

Dear Sirs of the international edition of EL PAIS, the only thing I ask of you is that you offer us more good news with greater frequency. Good things also happen in the world, and sometimes we need to be reminded that courage and human goodness exist in the middle of desperate situations.

I bid you goodbye wishing the international edition of EL PAIS all the happiness and long live that it deserves. My applause. Happy anniversary and many more to come.

The Extraordinary History of the Postal Service of Vanuatu

In December 1991, an article entitled 'Vanuatu and its historical stamps" that I had written for the Stamps and Coin Mart magazine, was published. Not that I am a stamp collector, but the subject seemed so interesting that I decided to write an article for lovers of the topic.

Here is the article.

The history of the Postal Service of Vanuatu in the South Pacific is not a common one.

Previously, the country was known as the New Hebrides, before its independence in 1980, and it used to be governed by England and France since 1906 when they created The Condominium of the New Hebrides.

The French wanted to take control of the New Hebrides from their base in New Caledonia, and the British the same from their bases in Fiji and Australia. This conflict of interests led to the creation of a joint administration that was called The Condominium of the New Hebrides.

This meant that everything was divided into two parts operating separately, including postage stamps: one edition in French and another in English. Before this, the people were accustomed to using stamps from other countries.

The first European explorer to reach the islands in May 1606 was Pedro Fernández de Quirós, a Portuguese captain working for the Spanish Crown. He named the first island that he discovered "Espiritu Santo", which it still conserves today.

Continuous dabbling and struggles with the natives forced Quirós to abandon the islands after 55 days. One century was then to pass before another group of explorers attempted to colonize the islands.

The English Capitan James Cook arrived in the islands in 1774, and named them the New Hebrides, like the Hebrides islands off the coast of Scotland.

French explorers also arrived. The legendary French explorer, Bougainville, reached them in 1768, and Laperouse, another famous French explorer, in 1778. However, both ships sank in the coral reefs during fierce storms, and there were no survivors to tell the tale. Two centuries more were to pass before the wrecks were discovered.

The islands were rich in Sandalwood, which was valuable merchandise in the Eighteenth Century. Whalers also arrived in the area, followed by traders, who landed in order to extract the Sandalwood trees from the forests.

The missionaries followed, determined to bring Christianity to the Melanesian inhabitants of the islands. A mixture of trade, fortune hunting, and religion attracted Europeans, who arrived to settle on the islands.

One of the first stamps to be used was produced by an Australian trading company called Burns Philp in 1897, when the company started operations on the islands. After the independence of the country in 1980 a set of bi-lingual stamps were introduced to better reflect the independent status and unity of the country.

In 1991, Vanuatu issued five different stamps for collectors. The topics covered reflect on the ni-Vanuatu people, the natural environment, and the achievements of the country.

The first stamp to be issued in January 1991 was dedicated to four species of precious butterflies. In May 1991, the theme for the stamp was the Second National Folklore Festival that took place in June 1991 on the island of Espiritu Santo. Indigenous people from all the different islands of Vanuatu met together to share dances and other ancestral customs.

In August 1991 the subject was meteorology, a very important topic for a country that regularly suffers natural disasters such as cyclones and earthquakes. In October 1991, the theme was birds. This was to mark the recent discovery of a rare species of marine bird on one of the islands of Vanuatu's first marine nature park. In December 1991, the stamp was dedicated to HIV/AIDS to join the global fights against the illness.

The stamps that are published are either definitive or commemorative editions, and of the 32,000 stamps printed, collectors in Britain and France purchase around 11,000.

A definitive edition comprises 15 different stamps,

and a commemorative edition has 4 different stamps. The majority of the stamp designs are produced in England with a few exceptions.

To commemorate the celebration of the 1991 National Folklore Festival, an edition of 4 stamps was issued. The festival was the second to be celebrated and will take place every ten years. The first festival took place before independence in 1980, and the second took place in June 1991 on the island of Espiritu Santo.

Apart from one stamp for 25 vatu (vatu is the currency of Vanuatu), which shows a ceremonial dance from the South East Malekula, the other stamps cover subjects that include more than one island.

The stamps on the subject of the festival were designed by Sue Wickison, an English resident of Vanuatu, whose main work for the previous nine years had been for the Kew Royal Botanical Gardens as an illustrator of new species of floral plants, and for other scientific papers.

For collectors around the world, the stamps of Vanuatu are a precious example of the fascinating events and things that can be found in this remote country.

When this article was published, the British High Commissioner asked Peter if I really was the author. Apparently, he was a stamp collector and was impressed that I had written this article in English. From then onwards, he never mentioned cheap Spanish wines again!

It's a Cyclone

As proof that paradise on earth does not exist, even in Vanuatu, there is inevitably some danger: cyclones!

I have experienced three cyclones during my time in Vanuatu, and I very well understand the fear and misfortunes caused by natural disasters. Even when people can be alerted in advance, this does not mean that they can be completely avoided.

Vanuatu is the South Pacific country with the highest propensity to suffer cyclones. Between 1970 and 1985, approximately 29 hurricanes and cyclones passed through Vanuatu. On average, each of the islands is hit by a cyclone every two years, normally between January and April. As a consequence of climate change affecting the planet, cyclones are increasingly frequent and more violent in recent years.

During the rainy season from November until April, there can be heavy rains at any moment, caused by a cyclone in the region. However, nothing is comparable with experiencing a cyclone hitting the area where one finds oneself.

When I arrived in Vanuatu in 1989, Cyclone Uma had caused great destruction in the capital, Port Vila, and swept away the coral reefs that ring this part of the country. Around the island of Hideaway, a short distance by boat from Port Vila, the coral had been completely destroyed, and it took two years before one could see the marvellous corals again, as they had been before the cyclone struck. In any case, everything grows and renews itself with time in Vanuatu. The ni-Vanuatu know that after the destruction, the vegetation and the coral will grow back again. Nothing disappears forever, except people.

The first experience I had of what it all meant was when officials of the British High Commission called us to a talk about how to best prepare for the arrival of a cyclone. The talk took place in a school classroom where the wind was blowing with such intensity as to shake the badly closed doors, portending the adventures of cyclones in arrival.

To start with, they told us that one has to prepare

the house in the event of a cyclone in order that, not only will the strong wind not blow away one's possessions, but also to protect them from the amount of water that comes along. For example, you have to put books inside plastic sacks and place them in locations away from the floor, as when the cyclone arrives, water invades the house. Fragile objects need to be safeguarded as the wind will blow strongly even inside the house, and one has to open the windows on the side of the house opposite to where the wind is blowing, in order to avoid the build up of pressure inside that would make the roof explode. Next, they told us that one has to put adhesive tape in the form of an X on the windows, so that if they break they will not fall in pieces. As a finishing touch about practicalities, one has to forget about using candles because the wind is so strong it would be useless to light them. The only lights that work are storm lanterns.

Imminent cyclone warnings are usually given some two or three days in advance, when it starts to rain as in the Great Flood. The sky starts to darken, and when the cyclone is on the point of arrival, the sky darkens during the day as if it were night, and the rain become a curtain of water that covers everything. Gradually, the electricity is cut off, and next, the radio messages stop, and, in darkness and silence, one prepares oneself for what may happen with anxious expectation.

Our first cyclone was the least terrible, more than anything because of our lack of knowledge about the phenomenon. Though I do remember that we spent the night bailing out with buckets owing to the quantity of water that entered through the crevices around the windows and doors even though we had covered them with old clothes. Peter made a comment about how was it possible that planes were allowed to fly with the imminent arrival of a cyclone. I replied that the loud noise was not a plane, but the sound of the cyclone as it approached Port Vila!

Some people, who love danger, and above all with a high level of disregard, or unawareness, for personal safety, dare to go out during a cyclone to experience what it feels like. They not only see trees flying around and twisting electricity poles, but also in the majority of cases, they get injured by some roofing sheets flying about, or, in the best of events, they manage to grasp anything available to avoid flying off like Mary Poppins. All this whilst soaked to the skin with the wind functioning like a blow dryer that instead of drying you, hoses you. The nest day, we discovered that some people had lost their houses, others the roofs of their houses, and the most fortunate, some trees in the garden. What we did not lose was our fear of cyclones, and we had to go through two more similar experiences.

The second cyclone caught us in a new house, which had special metal shutters to protect the windows from cyclones. We spent all night praying that the cyclone would pass, and we were too frightened to sleep. Nothing happened to us, although some other people could not say the same. Both expatriates and ni-Vanuatu lose their houses during cyclones. For the ni-Vanuatu all this forms part of the experiences of life, and it is not worthwhile crying for what one has lost, but one has to start to reconstruct as soon as possible, It is a brave and stoic attitude that I admire strongly. For me, when I was told that the house where we used to live had been destroyed, and the roof had been blown off, I felt frightened to think that this could have happened whilst we had been living there.

In these cases, human solidarity becomes commonplace. There is always someone with extra plates or furniture that can help a neighbour or a friend to reconstruct what they have lost. It is considered normal to help within one's possibilities.

About the third cyclone, I only remember that the wind was so strong that it became impossible to talk inside the house and be heard. We survived this one as well. We had a lot of luck whilst in Vanuatu. Now I prefer to remember cyclones as an experience in the past.

The Spanish Dancer

In Vanuatu, someone once told me that when you feel an unbearable pain in your soul, you should create an invisible thread with which to tie the pain around a stone and then throw the object into the sea. This is the story of a pain that lies on the bottom of a lagoon in the South Pacific.

With only a few months to go before leaving Vanuatu, after four years of unforgettable experiences, and on return from my father's funeral in Barcelona, I received a note and a calendar with paintings by the Dutch actor, Jerome Krabbé, who had been recently filming in Vanuatu, and who had spent his time between filming sessions on his favourite hobby, painting. Later he published a calendar with his work.

The note accompanying the calendar was from Leticia, also Dutch like the actor, who had returned to Vanuatu three years after the death of her husband in tragic circumstances. The note was very nice, and made me remember those moments when Leticia and her mother stayed in my house some days after the tragedy. After some years, Leticia had decided to return for two weeks to see the place where she had spent happy times, and also extreme sadness, and to say goodbye forever to that part of her life. I could not meet her as I was in Barcelona, but I felt intuitively that her wounds were cured.

A few months after I had arrived in Vanuatu, I joined a group of women that used to meet to sew, embroider and interchange techniques, and also to talk about our things and feel less alone so far away from home. It was called "The Sewing Group" and there I learned to express a part of me through quilting techniques that had never occurred to me whilst in Europe. Ever since, I have made several patchwork quilts that I always end up giving to my best friends. Leticia was part of this group, and was one of the youngest members. I had seen her two or three times there, but she was not a talkative person, apart from interchanging greetings and other comments about the place and the weather. I could not say that I knew her. I was aware that she was married to a Dutch man, who worked as an associate expert for the United Nations. Both were under 30, and recently married, when they had arrived in Vanuatu one year earlier.

On Saturday mornings, I usually went to the open-air market to buy some fruit and vegetables from the ni-Vanuatu women, who used to grow crops and sell them there. Afterwards, I used to head for 'La Tentation Café' where I would always find someone I knew with whom to share a table and have an entertaining chat. The café was open air, by the sea, and from the tables you had a view of Iririki Island.

That Saturday, I never reached 'La Tentation' because on the way I encountered Leticia's mother, who had travelled from Holland to attend her son-in-law's funeral. He had died in mysterious circumstances that I will recount later. I had briefly met this lady at the funeral, which was attended by the majority of Port Vila's expatriate population. I believe she was called Margaret, or something similar. I found her walking alone on the main street of Port Vila, and when I asked her about her daughter, she started crying. She told me that Leticia just stayed in bed since several days, not wanting to see anybody, not eating and just crying continuously. I offered to accompany her to the house and try to console Leticia, more than anything out of human solidarity in a desperate situation.

At first, Leticia refused to see me, but I managed to enter her room after lightly tapping on the door. We talked, I believe, for two hours. In the end, I left with the promise that she would get up, and come and stay at my house with her mother for the last four days of her remaining time in Vanuatu. I have to say that the person in the personnel department responsible for her husband at the United Nations in New York behaved in a very cold manner and without solidarity, not offering any type of support, or financial assistance, in those difficult and unpredictable times. In those fragile moments, both Leticia and her mother felt very vulnerable, and started to worry about the little money that they had left. This is how they ended up being my guests.

Once in my house, Leticia explained in detail what

had happened to her husband. It was a Sunday afternoon, and they had decided to spend some time on a small island that lies a bit over 100 metres from the Port Vila shore, and which can be reached by boat. Leticia's husband decided to swim across the stretch of water, and Leticia took the boat. An hour passed without any signs of her husband, and Leticia started to get worried, and began asking for help from the people at a small hotel and restaurant on the island. After several hours search by the authorities, the body of Alex, Leticia's husband, was not found. The misfortune was double for her since neither could they find the body of her husband, nor could she be certain of his death.

A Japanese tourist had disappeared in the same lagoon a couple of years earlier. The legends about the place bestowed a magic power on a dragon like snake which according to the locals lived in the submarine caves that surround the island, and that, every two or three years, exhorts a human sacrifice. Being Vanuatu, there were magicians sacrificing chickens and other creatures in their attempts to discover the fate of Alex, but with no results. One of the magicians said that Alex's spirit was at the bottom of the lagoon that encircled the island.

The days passed, and Leticia and her mother had to return to Holland. I saw Leticia smile when I bid her goodbye at Port Vila airport, and then I knew that some day she would manage to overcome the tragedy.

Months passed, and one day I decided to cross the lagoon with a friend in the same place where Alex had disappeared a few months before. Before boarding the boat in order to cross over the short distance to the island's shore, I saw a red-coloured creature with white specks the size of a plum that seemed to be calling my attention by moving in a strange way. When I paid closer attention, it started to contort itself and to move like a miniature manta ray. Mentioning this to my friend, it also caught her attention. As it was something unusual, my friend, who had spent several years living in Vanuatu, decided to consult one of her books about the creatures that inhabit those waters, and she found the name of the creature that we had seen a few hours before, moving its body by the shore as if it was doing a personalised performance. Carola called me, all excited, and told me that the name of the creature was Spanish Dancer, which explained its winding movements and the white specks on a red background. What is more, she said that it was very rare to see it by the shore, as normally it lives in the depths of the lagoon. I was astonished because I remembered what had been said about the spirits of the lagoon, and I thought that there was a hidden message in all this.

The nest day I received a letter from Leticia in which she thanked me for all I had done for her some months before, and asked me to pass on an envelope enclosed and addressed to Carola.

Could it be that the spirit of Alex inhabited that Spanish Dancer, which danced for us as if to say thank you, and also to let us know that he was fine and happy in the waters of the lagoon, and he was asking us to communicate this to Letizia? I will never know, but I have my own ideas.

Cannibals and Magicians

It is generally believed in 'civilized' countries that cannibalism and magic do not exist any more, and that they are just trickery aimed at the credulous. After having lived in Vanuatu for four years, I reserve judgement on this matter.

Officially, cannibalism disappeared from Vanuatu in the 1960s. It was an important part of the culture of the islands during thousands of years, and maybe it is due to the influence of the Christian missionaries that the majority of the tribes that populate the different islands of Vanuatu no longer consider this practice a desirable ritual. However, like nearly everything in Vanuatu, it is impossible to be sure one hundred per cent that the prohibition is totally effective. Although, it is certain that people do not give human arms and legs as presents any more, instead of the traditional poultry, when they come from the islands to visit the capital.

In 1917, the Big Nambas captured the adventurers, Osa and Martin Johnson, on the island of

Malekula, as they attempted to make a film about the island's tribes with the purpose of preserving a film record of a form of primitive lifestyle before it disappeared through civilization. They were lucky because before being devoured in a cannibal feast, a British ship arrived providentially, and they were able to escape by running away through the jungle. The film that resulted from this experience entitled 'Among the Cannibal Isles of the South Pacific' proved to be a great success. The Johnsons return to the South Pacific in 1919 with various members of their team to film the next film entitled 'Cannibals of the South Seas'. This time they were received cordially by the great chief of the Big Nambas, maybe because he was convinced they possessed magic powers, but overall because he was happy to receive the presents they brought. The island of Malekula is one of the most renowned islands for its complex megalithic culture and its ritual art forms associated with rites of initiation, graduation and status, plus certain types of secret societies and highly elaborated funeral rites. Malekula is the second largest island in Vanuatu with an extension of 2,069 square kilometres and a population of 24,000 people that speak 35 different languages, with a similar number of sub-dialects for these languages. In the majority of museum collections emanating from Vanuatu, half of the material originates from Malekula.

Even though the majority of the inhabitants in the interior of Malekula have converted to Christianity, a large part of the south of the island continues to be the centre of a complex spiritual world that recognises the influence of ancestral spirits. The tribes from those parts continue to practice rituals that connect the material world with the spiritual one using sacrifices, songs, dances, and by making characteristic art forms. It is a very complicated part of the world, and in the south of Malekula there still exist 21 different languages, as well as sub-dialects, for a population of 8,800 people. Each language area has cultural differences with its neighbours. Both linguistically and culturally, the south of Malekula is probably the most complex stretch of land on the planet.

Their beliefs include the certainty that, through

magic, they can transform themselves into sharks, and, as such, attack their enemies. This is a widespread belief in Vanuatu, and some shark attacks are treated as highly suspicious by the ni-Vanuatu, who believe that an enemy is behind them. A story used to circulate that took place in the 1980s about a Swiss travel agent, who decided to visit the island of Malekula with the intention of organising tours for European tourists to visit the tribes there. In spite of being warned about the ferocious tribes, the Big Nambas and the Small Nambas, that are not in favour of receiving tourists, the Swiss travel agent took no notice, and after arriving at the airport on Malekula on a small plane, saw that he was by the sea and decided to go for a bathe as it was hot. As soon as he was waist deep in the water, a shark appeared and no more was known about the Swiss travel agent. According to the ni-Vanuatu, he was attacked by an inhabitant of Malekula, who transformed himself into a shark to teach the man a lesson.

The magicians, or Klevers as they are known colloquially, produce magic potions in order to cure all types of illnesses, that are nearly always caused by an enemy who has, at the same time, contracted the services on another Klever. There are real cases of a rich, cultured and good-looking person being capable of abandoning literally everything for an unattractive, poor, and uneducated person as a result, people believe, of a magic spell cast by a klever. Klevers are, at once, both feared and respected. The expatriates do not have contact with this type of thing, but living in Vanuatu, we know that there is an underworld, to which the magic belongs.

In Vanuatu, people fear visiting certain islands because of the danger involved. Of all of the islands, perhaps the most feared is the island of Ambrym, considered to be the centre of Vanuatu's black magic. Ambrym is also known as having some of the best wooden sculptures in the South Pacific, and also for its mysterious Rom Dance. During the dance, the dancers wear colourful masks and they hide themselves beneath a cloak made of dried banana leaves. A giant gong made of carved wood, called a 'tam tam' provides the rhythmic sound that accompanies the chants and foot stamping of the dance. This dance is thousands of years old, and is still performed in the original way.

The majority of the 'tam tam' gongs are made from the timber of breadfruit trees, and it requires great patience and skill to make one. Only certain men have the right to carve a 'tam tam'. Currently, the majority of them portray ancient figures, and this gives them certain magic powers.

Ancient beliefs still have a place in Vanuatu, whose society was rated in July 2006, using a radical new index published by the New Economics Foundation (NEF) and Friends of the Earth, to be the happiest country on earth. The parameters used were: life expectancy, well-being and nature conservation. The ni-Vanuatu consider themselves to the guardians of the earth for future generations. The only things that worry them are cyclones and earthquakes. They take life in a light-hearted manner and do not worry unnecessarily. It is important for them to smile, and not leave other people feeling uncomfortable or upset. They have at least one of the secrets of happiness, and more happiness than countries that are richer and more civilized. That situation is, for me, the best magic that exists.

Myriam

The last time I saw Myriam was in December 1998 in a hospital in Paris. We had come to know each other some years before, when I arrived in Vanuatu and went to ask her for a job teaching Spanish at the University of the South Pacific, where she was the Director. We got on immediately, something rare for Myriam, who was accustomed to carefully selecting her friends, not out of snobbishness, but for survival.

Myriam was a rare bird, of which you only find one in a million. I had the great fortune to come to know her and become her friend. During the four years that I lived in Vanuatu, our friendship developed gradually, and we learned to mutually respect each other as we continued getting to know each other, and trusted each other with confidences that we did not find easy to share with other people.

We talked about our past, our dreams, our pains of existence, and a chateau in France where we wanted to create a forum for intercultural exchanges between young people across the world, so that they would get to know each other better, away for the stereotypes we are given, that separate us rather than unite us. Myriam and I had the dream of buying an old chateau that, with the help of our respective husbands (somewhat reluctantly for practical reasons), to create an oasis for the young people of the world. I believe that if the young at heart, not years, exist, Myriam and I would have joined for life.

As we got to know each other, I found out that she was the daughter of a three-star French general and a distinguished lady of the high society of Marseilles. She had two brothers and two sisters, and all carried wounds from a difficult childhood controlled by a mother who did not know how to be one. From the outside, she had a privileged position, but from the inside, her home was more like hell. The scars of a childhood without love affected each of the children in a different way.

Myriam was intelligent and had studied political science at the University of the Sorbonne in Paris.

Always looking for different perspectives and new adventures, she decided to write her doctoral thesis about New Caledonia, a French overseas territory, at an Australian university. Thanks to her position as the daughter of a general, she gained access to a series of semi-secret files from which she developed her thesis, later becoming a book, about France's policies towards New Caledonia. Her thesis dared, not only to suggest, but also to demonstrate, that the treatment of the kayaks (indigenous Melanesians) of New Caledonia represented racial segregation and other similar practices. This made her persona non grata for the French establishment. Her father received several telephone calls about it, suggesting that the education of his daughter lacked the essential elements of patriotism.

For Myriam, a free spirit, the opinions of the establishment were not as important as her quest for the truth and her efforts to create a better society than the one she had inherited.

In Vanuatu, Myriam met the man who would

become her husband, the ni-Vanuatu son of a famous tribal chief of one of the islands. He belonged to the equivalent of our aristocracy. He was also an intelligent person with a high-level human and university education. Myriam's father learnt to accept the decision of his daughter but not so her mother, who continued to treat him systematically more like her daughter's servant than her husband during the few occasions when they had to see each other. Myriam and Ricky had two sons, who became a part of his large family.

Myriam was appointed the director of the University of the South Pacific in Port Vila and was very respected by both students and lecturers as her style was humane and uninhibited whilst always seeking excellence for the Melanesian students, whom she encouraged to express the best of themselves.

She did not have friends amongst the expatriate French community, who felt intimidated by her intelligence and lack of snobbery. Her friends were few and all could be described as free spirits;

a person who had decided to be herself even going against certain hypocrisy in society.

The generosity of Myriam's soul was not common. As a loyal sister if ever there was one, she offered unconditional (and financial) help to her jailed brother in France, when he was arrested for armed assault to get money for his drugs fix, and no one else in the family wanted anything to do with him. Her generosity was dictated by the love she felt for her brothers, whom she understood, since she herself had been the victim of the psychological abuse of her mother and considered herself to be a fortunate survivor, whereas others had not been sufficiently strong or fortunate as her. .

Myriam maintained a close bond with one of her sisters, who married a miner and was looked down upon by her mother for her choice. As money was scarce in her sister's household, Myriam offered to pay the expenses for their vacation to visit Vanuatu and spend several weeks with her. Myriam was no millionaire, or anything like it, but she was conscious that with her salary and that of her husband they could afford more than her sister's family. If money has a purpose, it has to be to make us happy, and Myriam was happy to see her sister and family.

On the other hand, Myriam attracted envy. It was her generous spirit and bravery in the face of life that caused insecurity and a sense of inferiority in some people with less courage than her. The more she helped, the more they would criticise her behind her back. An example of this was a European woman married to a ni-Vanuatu man of humble means, who asked Myriam for financial assistance to set up a business. She was, for Myriam, a friend in need, and she did not give it a second thought. Some years later, the aforementioned person, now the owner of a prosperous business, criticised Myriam saying "of course, she can afford to help others without the need to remind them about the money they owe her." Later on, Myriam mentioned to me that the same person had not repaid her any part of the amount she had lent her, though she had decided not to pursue the matter in order not to create problems in their friendship. I decided to start with a clean slate with regard to that person, and remain loyal to my friendship with Myriam.

When a few years later, Myriam and her family visited us in Barcelona, we went for a stroll along Las Ramblas to show them this very symbolic part of the city where I grew up. At the start of our walk, at the Canaletas fountain, Myriam suddenly became petrified, and also her husband. Suddenly, I saw the figure of a man with Melanesian features with whom they exchanged friendly greetings, but somewhat coldly, like with someone you were not expecting to see, and you are taken by surprise.

Later, she commented that the man was a well-known kayak (Melanesian) from New Caledonia where she was living when she was writing her doctoral thesis. During her stay in Noumea, the capital of New Caledonia, Myriam fell ill and the doctors could not find anything wrong with her. Someone suggested that she visit a local witch doctor, who told her that there was a person who wished her dead. He promised to cure her on the condition that she never return to New Caledonia because, if so, she was at risk of losing her life. Myriam, as sceptical about these things as anyone could be, decided that if he had cured her then there must be a reason, and as in the old saying in Spanish about witches (meigas) "I don't believe in them, but having them there, they exist", she decided not to return to New Caledonia just in case.

To live in the South Pacific changes your perspective on things. In a certain way, it widens your view of the horizon, and it makes you understand that we cannot take in everything however wise we think we are. Myriam understood this and so did I.

Two years after I received a telephone call from Myriam from Paris where she was under treatment for cancer. She scolded me in a friendly manner for not having visited her in Fiji where she had been living in recent years for work reasons, and she asked me to visit her in Paris because she was due to be operated fairly soon, and wanted to see me.

I already knew from her emails that Myriam was following a treatment to recover from breast cancer and I had not given it more importance than this, because it was a therapy for an illness that is more or less under control these days. However, something about Myriam's call made a mark, and I immediately wanted to go to Paris to be with her after her operation and spend time chatting in a lively way whilst helping her pass away the boring hours of an enforced stay in hospital.

That call from Myriam was the last time I spoke with her. Some days later, I arrived in a grey and rainy Paris, and went directly to the apartment of Myriam's sister, who had offered to accompany me to the hospital. Talking to Isabelle, I understood that the situation was grave. She told me that Myriam had not regained consciousness after the operation and was connected by a tube to a respirator.

I arrived at the hospital and when I entered the room where Myriam was, an electric shock ran through my whole body. She lay with her eyes closed and her mouth was filled by the tube that provided her with oxygen, allowing her only to breathe but nothing else. I felt the urge to cry, and I realised that I was not as strong as I would have liked to be. Her sister, Isabelle, encouraged me to speak to her, but I could not do so. I left the room with tears streaming down my face.

I met the rest of Myriam's brothers and sisters in the hospital waiting room. They had come together on this very painful occasion for all of them, but not so her mother, who had spurned all contact with her daughter without clear reason, even knowing she was on the point of death. I left Paris knowing that I would never see Myriam again.

A few days before Christmas, we received that call from Ricky in Paris to inform us of Myriam's death. The funeral service took place in Vanuatu with a supportive congregation of people of different races and religions sharing a common feeling of sadness for the loss of an exceptional human being. There were many people who spoke about different important moments in Myriam's life. I could not be there, but my spirit was present that day.

Myriam is buried on an island in Vanuatu that I hope to be able to visit in the future. In Vanuatu, the people have exceptional memories, and remember every little detail of the life of a person with whom they have had contact. For Myriam, to be remembered is her passport to eternity. When someone remembers us with affection, we do not die entirely.

One house in Malapoa and another in Tassiriki

When I feel a little sad, or off form, I try to remember the first house where I lived in Vanuatu, and when I remember my tropical garden and those marvellous views of Irirki Island, surrounded by the yachts that were arriving in the bay of Port Vila, my problems magically disappear.

I had two different houses in Vanuatu. The house in Malapoa is the one that brings me the most affectionate memories as the scene of our first period in Vanuatu, and of so many experiences with unforgettable people in a uniquely memorable setting.

Upon arrival in Vanuatu, we stayed at a hotel, managed by an Australian family, near the centre of Port Vila. Almost immediately, I started making efforts to find a house in order to create a more permanent home. At the time, there was a shortage of comfortable houses, although it was not impossible to find one after an intense search. For this reason, when they told me that there was a house available on Malapoa hill, some three kilometres from Port Vila, I did not hesitate to go and see it.

It was love at first sight when I visited it for the first time, and it was to be my home in Vanuatu for two years. Just going up the stairs from the garden to the main door, I could see the marvellous view that extended out in front of the terrace where one could see the tropical lagoon with Iririki Island in the middle, surrounded by yachts arriving in Port Vila. Before entering the house, I knew that this was to be my home in Vanuatu. We only spent a few days before moving there from the hotel where we were temporarily residing.

The house had bee uninhabited for more than a year. It had a swimming pool with views across Iririki Lagoon. The swimming pool was dirty and with the paint peeling off, just like the blue-grey facade of the house with its wooden ceiling. However, the views were extraordinary, and the garden was a splendid tropical paradise, full of fruit trees, and flowering plants of all sizes and colours that surrounded the swimming pool where one could swim whilst observing the fantastic view.

There was a huge mango tree at the entrance, but I can assure you that during the two years I lived there, I never eat any of its mangos. The ni-Vanuatu children from the house across the street were the first to pick them as soon as they were on the point of being ripe. As they had been doing this long before we came to live at the house, I did not want to create any problems and so I pretended I was unaware, thus allowing them to harvest the delicious fruit of that tree.

The gardener, who looked after the garden, had his own ideas about how to care for it, and in the first week, he cut the hibiscus plants, that acted as a hedge with the houses in front and on the side, down to their roots. I raised the roof when I saw it, but he excused himself by saying that they would grow back even more strongly! To be sure, he was right, and in a few weeks, we had large hibiscus shrubs with many flowers.

We had two beautiful frangipani trees, which offered us a wonderful fragrance when we were seated on the terrace. Frangipani flowers are traditionally used across the South Pacific to make garlands of flowers that are placed around the necks of guests as a sign of welcome. They are also called Tiare flowers in Tahiti. Inside houses, they are placed all over bathrooms and bedrooms as an air freshener because they give off a soft delightful perfume.

The sunsets one could see from our terrace were of incomparable beauty. The sky slowly changed to red and opened up to let through the glowing sun as it shone its last few rays of the day before going to rest, and handing over to the rising moon. Spending the early evening contemplating this marvellous spectacle became a ritual for us, and for our guests, when we had some. Not having television, the evenings and nights turned into parties or dinners in someone's house. There were always interesting conversations and there was, nearly always, someone new who had been invited the same day.

In Vanuatu, we spent four years without television, as it did not exist there in that period, and the news always arrived with some delay. My subscription to the newspaper El Pais Internacional always arrived at least three weeks after the date of publication, when it travelled on time. I missed many news stories, but I must be honest, I learnt that often one lives better with less news broadcasts, talking more to other people, and living out in the fresh air. I cannot say that I missed television. I learnt a lot without it.

The parties were amazing. I can say, without any doubt, that I have not had occasion since then to go to parties so well prepared and entertaining as the ones we had in Vanuatu. I remember a party in a colonial mansion at the top of a hill with views that left you breathless, plus the best French champagne and exquisite food using a mixture of French and ni-Vanuatu recipes with enormous shrimps and delicious fish caught fresh that day for the party, and there was also an orchestra paying tropical rhythms as the sun slowly set.

In my house, I organised intimate parties with entertaining anecdotes. One in particular appeared to me to have been taken from a tale of black humour. We had met an Argentinian couple shortly after our arrival, and they had been instrumental in introducing us to other people, with whom we had in turn established a friendship. Klaus and Martina were charming and good hosts and recounted curious and entertaining anecdotes based on their experiences in different countries. Only once was I on the point of arguing with Klaus when he told me that the Spaniards were unlucky because of the loss of Franco. I tried to change the subject more than anything because I could see myself arguing with him over the mistakenness of his views. After that, a little doubt stayed with me about Klaus.

It was at a party in my house that my intuition was confirmed. Klaus' mother had come from Argentina to spend some weeks with her son and daughter-in-law, and I also invited her to the party. The lady was nearly eighty and I believe her memory was starting to fail. However, when she told me that Klaus had needed to change his surname in order to work for a well-known international organization, I understood that maybe his German origins had something to do with his arrival in Argentina at the end of the

1940s. I pretended I had not heard what she had said, and lucky for me, Klaus arrived and took her to somewhere else in the party. So maybe Klaus was the son of an escaped Nazi? My imagination took flight.

On the other hand, there were other Germans who had been residing in Vanuatu for many years. Although they would never admit it, I could swear that they were Nazis from Hitler's time. After all, Vanuatu is the antipodes of Europe. One lady in particular treated her ni-Vanuatu staff as if she were running a concentration camp. I don't know what happened to her, but the ni-Vanuatu never forget an offense against them, and even if many years pass, they always take their revenge.

Our Malapoa house was also the scene of a marvellous New Year's Eve party that ended cruelly. We were several hours ahead of Barcelona due to the time difference, and I had spoken with my parents a few hours earlier when they had called to wish me a happy new year. Whilst I was tidying up the leftovers from the party, the phone rang, but this time I heard the faltering voice of my mother, who informed me that my father had passed away a few hours after midnight in Barcelona. There are various painful experiences in my life that I keep stored away in a locked drawer, whose key I threw as strongly as I could into the sea, and this is one of the most painful. After two hours, I left for Barcelona via the Solomon Islands and Thailand, the only route available at that moment. I took more than two days to arrive, which is too long to attend a normal funeral, that has to take place within one day of the death, but my uncle moved heaven and earth to obtain a delay so that I could arrive before my father was buried. My uncle also died from cancer one year later, a little before my return to Barcelona.

I arrived at Barcelona airport physically and emotionally exhausted after more than 28 hours of flights. I only had time to put on the coat that my brother-in-law had brought to the airport. From there we went to the funeral and the burial that I still remember like a bad dream that is difficult to wake from. I saw faces and people, who spoke to me, but I was only slightly aware. The memory remains with me of being able to speak with my father a few hours before his death, and I remember his beautiful words, said with love: "Take good care of yourselves as you are so fay away. You know that we love you and we are looking forward to seeing you for the Barcelona Olympics." My father died on the 1st of January 1992. I saw the opening ceremony of the Olympic games on a video that's some friends sent to Vanuatu for me, and my eyes filled with tears. I did not return to Barcelona until after the games.

It was in the Malapoa house that I experienced my first cyclone. As I have already recounted, I remember that we spent the night bailing out water with buckets. The water got into every nook and cranny in the house. However, as it was our first cyclone, we waited for it expectantly, because of the novelty. Though after we had experienced one, we did not want to have any more first-hand knowledge of cyclones, but later in the new house, we would face two more.

Unfortunately, after two years living there, we had serious water problems, and it was necessary to move house. This time we went to live in a newly built house in the area of Port Vila called Tassiriki from where one could see the other lagoon, called Erakor. The house was attractive and comfortable, but it did not have either the years or the charm of the previous one. It was a little bit larger and it had enormous terraces, but the views were not comparable, although yes, it did have views overlooking a tropical lagoon! Sine that time, I give a lot of importance to living somewhere with as beautiful views as possible. I am willing to sacrifice other things in a house for that.

In this second house, I organized one of the best parties of my life, and I have done many. It was the party for Peter's 40th birthday. A Polynesian friend, who was a dancer, offered to perform some Polynesian dances during the party with three of her friends, who were also dancers. These were authentic Polynesian dances in the South Pacific! The historical restaurant, Rossi, prepared the buffet in which the famous roasted pig had to be present. The expatriates and ni-Vanuatu guests numbered about one hundred. A group of ni-

Vanuatu musicians entertained the party guests with traditional music. It was a fantastic party in the incomparable setting of my house in the South Pacific in front of a lagoon with South Pacific island dancers performing in their natural element.

Although several years have passed, I am sure that there are people who still remember that night. For sure, the ni-Vanuatu will do so, as they don't forget anything. Years can pass by, but they still remember all the details that the majority of people have forgotten.

One month before we were due to leave Vanuatu definitively; someone poisoned my faithful dog, Whistle, who had been with us since our arrival in Port Vila. An English couple that were leaving the country had given her to us. They had always kept her in the garden, not allowing her inside the house. I let her come inside, and she showed me a lot of affection, following me everywhere, and becoming my protector. I never had a guard dog so loyal and protective. We buried her under a tree in the garden. The tree was a Flaming Tree, named after the colour of its vibrant red flowers that bloom at a certain time of year. According to the ni-Vanuatu, this tree protects the spirits of the dead, and helps them to rest in peace.

We left Vanuatu in June 1993 on a splendid tropical morning, sent off by a large number of friends, some of whom we will never see again. The memories have never faded. I hope to return some day.

Index

1. Foreword 5
2. Introduction 11
3. Acknowledgements 14
4. Welcome to Paradise 16
5. The French, the English and the
   Natives – Together but not mixed 24
6. The British Ambassador 33
7. A toast with kava and other Melanesian customs .. 39
8. Southern Land of the Holy Spirit (Espiritu Santo).. 52
9. The Island of Pentecost and Bungee Jumping 61
10. The island of Tanna and its volcano 66
11. Contrasts from Vanuatu 75
12. The Extraordinary History of the Postal
    Service of Vanuatu 80
13. It's a Cyclone 86
14. The Spanish Dancer 92
15. Cannibals and Magicians 99
16. Myriam 117
17. One house in Malapoa and another in Tassiriki .. 117

If you wish to contact the author,
please send an email to mercy1924@yahoo.com

www.ingramcontent.com/pod-product-compliance
Lightning Source LLC
Chambersburg PA
CBHW071129090426
42736CB00012B/2063